Ways To Use AI In Business

by Dev Pin

Table of Contents

Introduction to AI in Business

Artificial Intelligence (AI) has fundamentally transformed the business landscape in recent years, ushering in a new era of innovation, efficiency, and competitiveness across industries. With its sophisticated algorithms and machine learning capabilities, AI has enabled businesses to harness the power of data like never before, leading to unprecedented opportunities for growth and optimization.

One of the key advantages of AI in business is its ability to revolutionize decision-making processes. By analyzing vast volumes of data and identifying patterns, AI systems can provide valuable insights that support strategic decision-making. From predicting consumer behavior to optimizing supply chain operations, AI-powered tools offer businesses a competitive edge by guiding them towards more informed and effective choices.

Moreover, the automation capabilities of AI have streamlined routine tasks and processes, allowing organizations to reallocate resources towards more strategic initiatives. Virtual assistants, chatbots, and robotic process automation tools have become indispensable in enhancing operational efficiency and reducing costs. Through the integration of AI technologies, businesses can enhance productivity, improve customer service, and drive overall performance.

In addition to operational benefits, AI plays a crucial role in enhancing customer experiences. By leveraging AI-driven personalization techniques, businesses can tailor their products and services to meet the specific needs and preferences of individual customers. This approach not only enhances customer satisfaction but also fosters brand loyalty and long-term relationships.

Furthermore, AI has revolutionized marketing and sales strategies by enabling businesses to deliver targeted and personalized campaigns. Through predictive analytics and machine learning algorithms, companies can identify potential leads, optimize pricing strategies, and forecast market trends with unprecedented accuracy. This data-driven approach to sales and marketing helps companies stay ahead of the competition and adapt quickly to changing market dynamics.

Despite its myriad benefits, the adoption of AI in business also presents ethical and societal challenges. Issues such as algorithmic bias, data privacy concerns, and the potential impact on the workforce require careful consideration. Businesses must prioritize ethical AI practices, ensure transparency in their algorithms, and establish frameworks for responsible AI implementation to build trust with consumers and mitigate potential risks.

In conclusion, the integration of AI technology in business represents a paradigm shift in how organizations operate, innovate, and compete in the digital age. By leveraging the capabilities of AI, businesses can unlock new possibilities, drive sustainable growth, and create value for stakeholders. Embracing AI is not just a strategic imperative but a necessity for businesses looking to thrive in an ever-evolving, data-driven marketplace.

Ways to use AI in Business

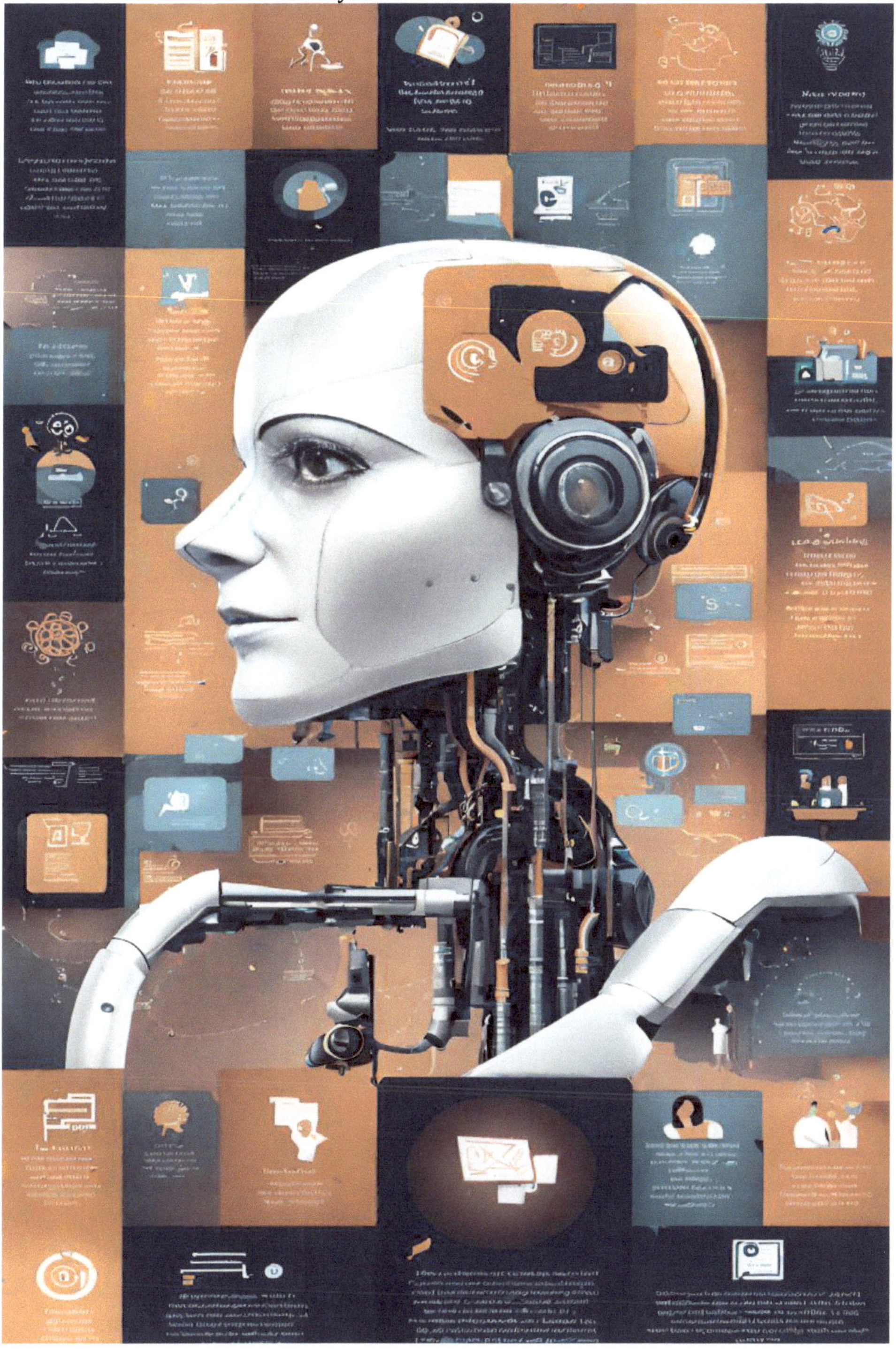

Understanding the Basics of Artificial Intelligence

Artificial Intelligence (AI) is a transformative field that encompasses a broad array of technologies and methodologies designed to replicate human intelligence and cognitive functions in machines. At its core, AI aims to enable machines to learn from experience, adapt to new inputs, and perform tasks that traditionally require human intervention. The multidisciplinary nature of AI draws on concepts from computer science, mathematics, psychology, neuroscience, and other disciplines to create intelligent systems capable of emulating various aspects of human intelligence.

Machine learning, a subset of AI, empowers algorithms to improve their performance over time by learning from data without being explicitly programmed. This approach has revolutionized industries such as healthcare, finance, and marketing by enabling machines to uncover patterns, make predictions, and optimize decision-making processes autonomously. Deep learning, a sophisticated form of machine learning that utilizes artificial neural networks to process complex data, has driven unprecedented breakthroughs in image and speech recognition, natural language processing, and autonomous driving.

Natural language processing (NLP) is a critical area of AI focused on enabling machines to comprehend and interact with human language effectively. NLP applications have reshaped communication interfaces, enabling voice-activated assistants, chatbots, and language translation tools to streamline interactions between humans and machines. With advancements in NLP models like transformer architectures and pre-trained language models, AI systems can generate coherent text, summarize information, and extract insights from vast amounts of textual data.

Computer vision is another vital component of AI that enables machines to analyze and understand visual information from images and videos. Through techniques like object detection, image segmentation, and facial recognition, computer vision systems can interpret and process visual data with remarkable accuracy. Applications of computer vision span diverse industries, from augmented reality and autonomous drones to medical imaging and industrial automation, driving significant advancements in safety, efficiency, and innovation.

Reinforcement learning, a dynamic approach within AI, involves training agents to make sequential decisions by interacting with an environment and receiving feedback on their actions. This technique has yielded impressive results in tasks like game playing, robotics, and optimization problems, where agents learn optimal strategies through trial and error. By combining reinforcement learning with deep learning and other AI methodologies, researchers have achieved groundbreaking results in complex decision-making scenarios, paving the way for autonomous systems that can learn and adapt in real-world environments.

The ethical implications of AI development and deployment are a pressing concern in the field. Issues such as algorithmic bias, data privacy, fairness, and transparency raise fundamental questions about the ethical use and societal impact of AI technologies. Ethical frameworks, regulations, and industry standards are crucial to ensuring that AI systems are developed and deployed responsibly, with due consideration for human values, rights, and well-being.

In conclusion, the continued advancement of AI technologies holds immense promise for addressing complex challenges and driving innovation across industries. By understanding the foundational principles and key applications of AI, businesses and organizations can leverage intelligent automation, data-driven insights, and enhanced decision-making capabilities to unlock new opportunities for growth, efficiency, and societal benefit. The intersection of AI with other transformative technologies like cloud computing, big data analytics, and the Internet of Things (IoT) opens up new possibilities for creating a more intelligent, connected, and innovative future.

Enhancing Customer Experiences with AI

In today's competitive business landscape, providing exceptional customer experiences is crucial for building brand loyalty and driving revenue growth. With the advancement of Artificial Intelligence (AI) technology, businesses have a powerful tool at their disposal to enhance and personalize customer interactions.

AI enables businesses to collect and analyze vast amounts of customer data in real-time, allowing for a deeper understanding of customer preferences and behaviors. By leveraging AI-powered tools such as chatbots, virtual assistants, and recommendation engines, businesses can provide personalized and timely responses to customer inquiries, leading to a more streamlined and efficient customer service experience.

One of the key benefits of using AI to enhance customer experiences is the ability to deliver personalized recommendations and offers based on individual customer preferences and behaviors. By analyzing past purchases, browsing history, and demographic information, AI algorithms can predict customer needs and preferences, allowing businesses to tailor their marketing and sales efforts to better meet the needs of their customers.

Furthermore, AI can help businesses improve the overall customer journey by identifying pain points and areas for improvement. By analyzing customer feedback and sentiment data, businesses can gain valuable insights into areas where they can make operational improvements to enhance the overall customer experience.

Moreover, AI-driven tools can enable businesses to implement proactive customer service strategies, where issues can be identified and resolved before they escalate, leading to higher customer satisfaction rates. By employing AI in customer service operations, businesses can also enhance their omnichannel customer experience, providing a consistent and seamless interaction across various touchpoints.

Additionally, AI can empower businesses to personalize marketing campaigns and offers, targeting customers with relevant content and promotions that are more likely to resonate with their preferences. By leveraging AI to analyze customer behaviors and engagement patterns, businesses can optimize their marketing efforts to drive higher conversion rates and customer engagement.

Moreover, AI can assist in automating routine tasks, freeing up human employees to focus on high-value interactions and strategic decision-making. Through machine learning algorithms, AI can continuously refine its understanding of customer behavior and preferences, allowing businesses to stay ahead of evolving customer needs and market trends.

Furthermore, with the integration of AI in customer experience, businesses can gain valuable insights from unstructured data sources such as social media, emails, and customer reviews. This data can be analyzed to detect trends, sentiment, and emerging issues, enabling businesses to proactively address customer concerns and drive continuous improvement in their products and services.

By harnessing AI to enhance customer experiences, businesses can create a competitive advantage by delivering personalized, efficient, and proactive interactions that meet the evolving expectations of today's consumers. As AI continues to advance and evolve, its potential to transform customer experiences and drive business growth remains unparalleled in the modern digital age.

Improving Operational Efficiency through Automation

In today's rapidly evolving business landscape, the relentless pursuit of operational efficiency has become a cornerstone of success for organizations striving to navigate a fiercely competitive marketplace. Amidst the ever-growing complexities of modern business operations, automation stands out as a transformative force that holds the promise of reshaping traditional paradigms and revolutionizing the way organizations function. Through the strategic integration of cutting-edge technologies such as artificial intelligence (AI) and machine learning, automation emerges as a pivotal driver of innovation, productivity, and competitive advantage.

At the heart of automation's disruptive potential lies its capacity to automate routine, mundane tasks that have traditionally consumed significant time and resources within organizations. By leveraging AI-powered automation solutions, businesses can streamline a myriad of processes, spanning from data entry and document processing to supply chain management and customer support. This not only liberates employees from the burdensome drudgery of repetitive tasks but also empowers them to focus on strategic, high-impact initiatives that demand human ingenuity and creative problem-solving.

Furthermore, automation empowers organizations to adapt swiftly to dynamic market dynamics and evolving customer demands. By harnessing intelligent systems capable of processing vast datasets in real-time, businesses can leverage actionable insights to make informed decisions rapidly, enabling them to stay ahead of the curve in a landscape where agility and responsiveness are decisive factors in achieving sustainable growth and market leadership.

The cost-saving implications of automation are profound. By automating labor-intensive processes, businesses can realize significant reductions in operational expenditures while simultaneously enhancing efficiency and accuracy across their operations. Moreover, the reduction of errors and rework facilitated by automation leads to improved product quality and heightened customer satisfaction, underscoring the broader value proposition that automation offers to organizations seeking to enhance their market competitiveness and customer loyalty.

However, the successful deployment of automation requires a comprehensive, methodical approach. Organizations must conduct a thorough evaluation of their existing processes, identify ripe opportunities for automation, and select appropriate tools and technologies that align with their unique requirements and strategic goals. Equally essential is the investment in the training and upskilling of employees to maximize the potential of automation solutions, addressing concerns related to job displacement and fostering a culture of technological proficiency and adaptability.

In summary, the pursuit of operational efficiency through automation has emerged as a critical imperative for organizations committed to achieving sustainable growth and staying ahead of the curve in an environment characterized by relentless change and disruption. By embracing the transformative capabilities of AI and automation technologies, businesses can unlock untapped potential, drive cost efficiencies, enhance decision-making capabilities, and deliver unparalleled value propositions to their customers. Automation is no longer a discretionary luxury but an essential catalyst for innovation, agility, and long-term success in a landscape defined by accelerating technological advancements and dynamic market forces.

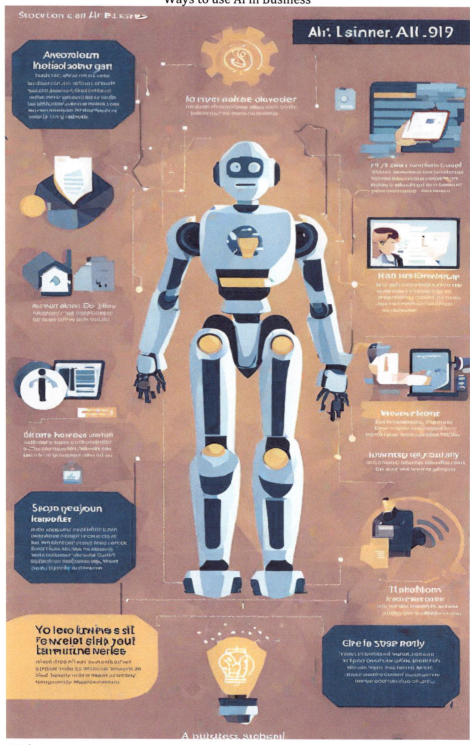

Leveraging AI for Data Analysis and Decision-Making

In today's highly competitive business landscape, data analysis and decision-making play a crucial role in driving success and maintaining a competitive edge. With the advancements in artificial intelligence (AI), organizations now have powerful tools at their disposal to leverage vast amounts of data for insightful analysis and informed decision-making.

AI algorithms and machine learning techniques have revolutionized the way data is processed and analyzed. By utilizing AI tools, businesses can uncover hidden patterns, trends, and insights from their data that would be difficult, if not impossible, to identify through traditional methods.

One of the key benefits of leveraging AI for data analysis is the ability to process and analyze large datasets quickly and efficiently. AI algorithms can sift through massive amounts of data within seconds, providing businesses with real-time insights that can inform decision-making processes in a timely manner.

Moreover, AI can identify correlations and predictive patterns within the data, enabling businesses to anticipate trends and make proactive decisions based on accurate forecasts. This predictive capability can help organizations mitigate risks, seize opportunities, and stay ahead of the competition.

AI-powered data analysis also provides businesses with a more holistic view of their operations and customer behaviors. By integrating data from various sources, AI can create a unified view of the business, allowing organizations to gain a deeper understanding of their performance and market trends.

Furthermore, AI can automate the decision-making process by providing intelligent recommendations and suggestions based on data analysis. This can help businesses streamline their decision-making processes, reduce human error, and make more informed and data-driven decisions.

The integration of AI in data analysis also opens up new possibilities for personalized marketing and customer engagement. By analyzing customer data, AI can help businesses tailor their marketing strategies to individual preferences, behaviors, and needs, leading to more effective and targeted campaigns.

Additionally, AI-driven data analysis can enhance risk management practices within organizations. By analyzing historical data and identifying potential risks, AI can help businesses proactively address and mitigate threats, reducing the likelihood of costly disruptions or crises.

Moreover, the evolution of AI in data analysis has significantly increased the scalability and accessibility of advanced analytics. With AI-driven tools, businesses of all sizes can leverage the benefits of sophisticated data analysis, enabling better decision-making processes and strategic planning.

Furthermore, AI can enhance data security practices by identifying anomalies and potential threats in real-time. This proactive approach to cybersecurity can help businesses safeguard their sensitive information and protect their systems from cyberattacks and breaches.

AI-powered data analysis can also drive innovation within organizations by uncovering new market opportunities, guiding product development initiatives, and improving operational efficiencies. By harnessing the power of AI, businesses can stay agile, adapt to changing market conditions, and drive sustainable growth in the long run.

In conclusion, the integration of AI in data analysis has transformative implications for businesses across industries. By leveraging AI-powered tools and techniques, organizations can unlock the full potential of their data assets, drive strategic decision-making, and enhance their competitive advantage in today's data-driven economy.

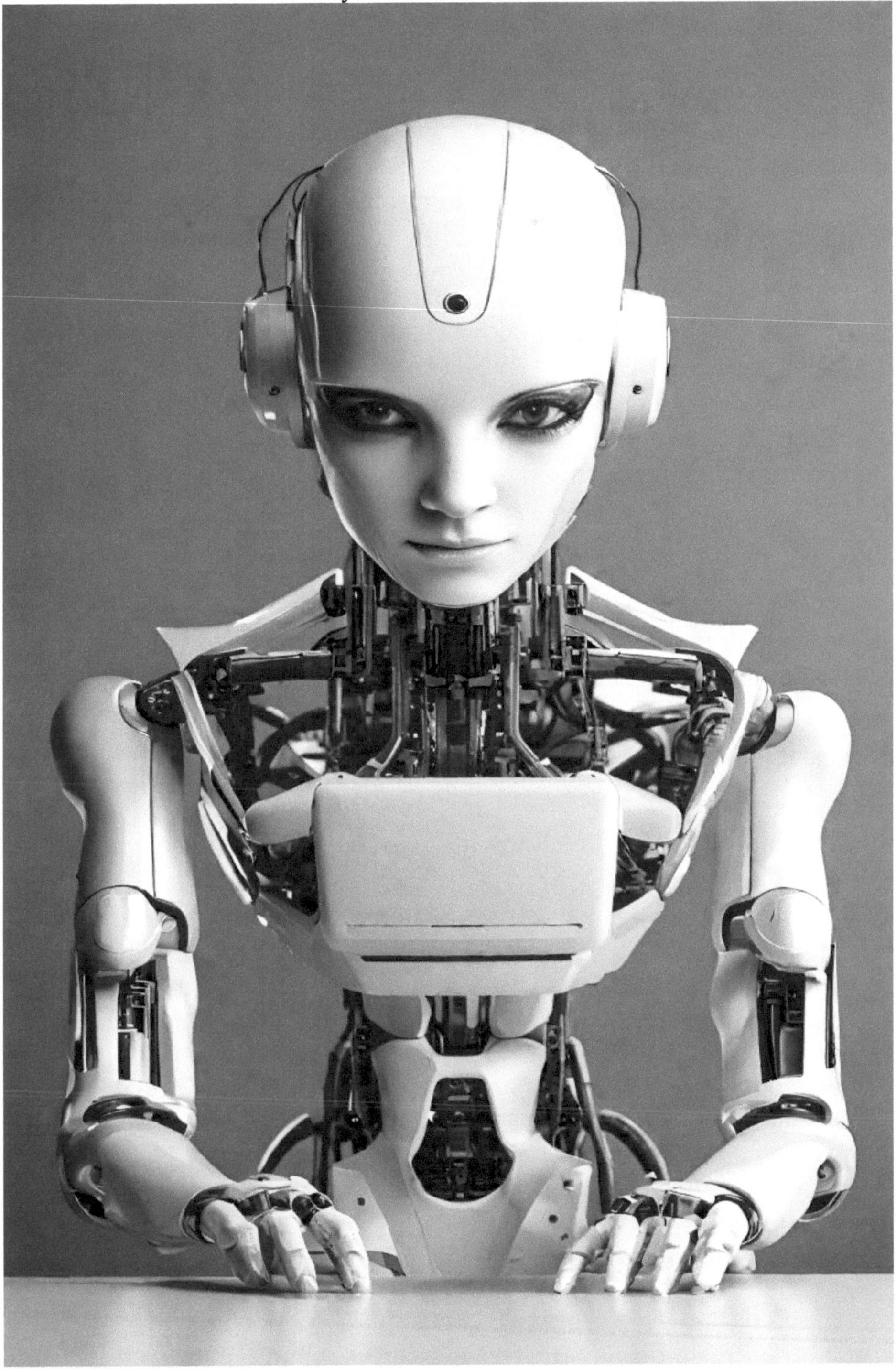

Implementing AI in Marketing and Sales Strategies

In today's fast-paced and competitive business landscape, implementing artificial intelligence (AI) in marketing and sales strategies has become increasingly crucial for companies looking to stay ahead of the curve. AI technologies offer a wide range of benefits that can help organizations streamline their processes, enhance customer engagement, and drive revenue growth.

One key area where AI can make a significant impact is in customer segmentation and targeting. By leveraging AI algorithms to analyze customer data and behavior patterns, businesses can gain valuable insights into their target audience and create more personalized marketing campaigns. This targeted approach not only improves the relevance of marketing messages but also increases conversion rates and customer satisfaction.

Moreover, AI-powered tools can automate various marketing tasks, such as email marketing, social media management, and online advertising. These automation tools enable companies to reach their target audience more efficiently and effectively, while also freeing up valuable time for marketing teams to focus on strategic planning and creativity.

In the realm of sales, AI technologies can revolutionize the lead generation and conversion processes. By using predictive analytics and machine learning algorithms, businesses can identify the most promising leads and prioritize sales efforts towards them. This targeted approach not only increases sales efficiency but also boosts the chances of conversion.

Furthermore, AI can empower sales teams with real-time insights and recommendations to better engage with customers and close deals. By analyzing customer interactions, preferences, and purchasing behavior, AI-powered tools can provide sales representatives with personalized recommendations and strategies for each individual prospect, ultimately leading to more successful sales outcomes.

In today's data-driven world, AI is becoming increasingly integrated into marketing and sales strategies to drive meaningful results. With the ability to analyze vast amounts of data in real-time, AI empowers companies to make informed decisions, predict customer behavior, and optimize their marketing and sales efforts.

By leveraging AI, businesses can also enhance customer experiences through personalized interactions and tailored messaging. AI-powered chatbots, for example, can provide instant customer support and assistance, while recommendation engines can suggest products or services based on individual preferences and past behavior.

Additionally, AI can help businesses optimize their pricing strategies, forecast demand, and identify opportunities for upselling and cross-selling. By analyzing pricing trends, competitor data, and customer feedback, AI algorithms can recommend optimal pricing structures to maximize profitability and customer satisfaction.

Moreover, AI plays a crucial role in analyzing marketing campaign performance, identifying areas for improvement, and refining strategies for future success. Through A/B testing, sentiment analysis, and performance tracking, businesses can continuously optimize their marketing efforts to drive higher returns on investment and better engagement with their target audience.

In conclusion, the integration of AI in marketing and sales strategies is not just a trend but a transformative force that has the potential to revolutionize how companies engage with customers, drive sales, and achieve business growth in today's competitive landscape. Embracing AI technologies is essential for businesses looking to stay agile, innovative, and customer-centric in the digital age.

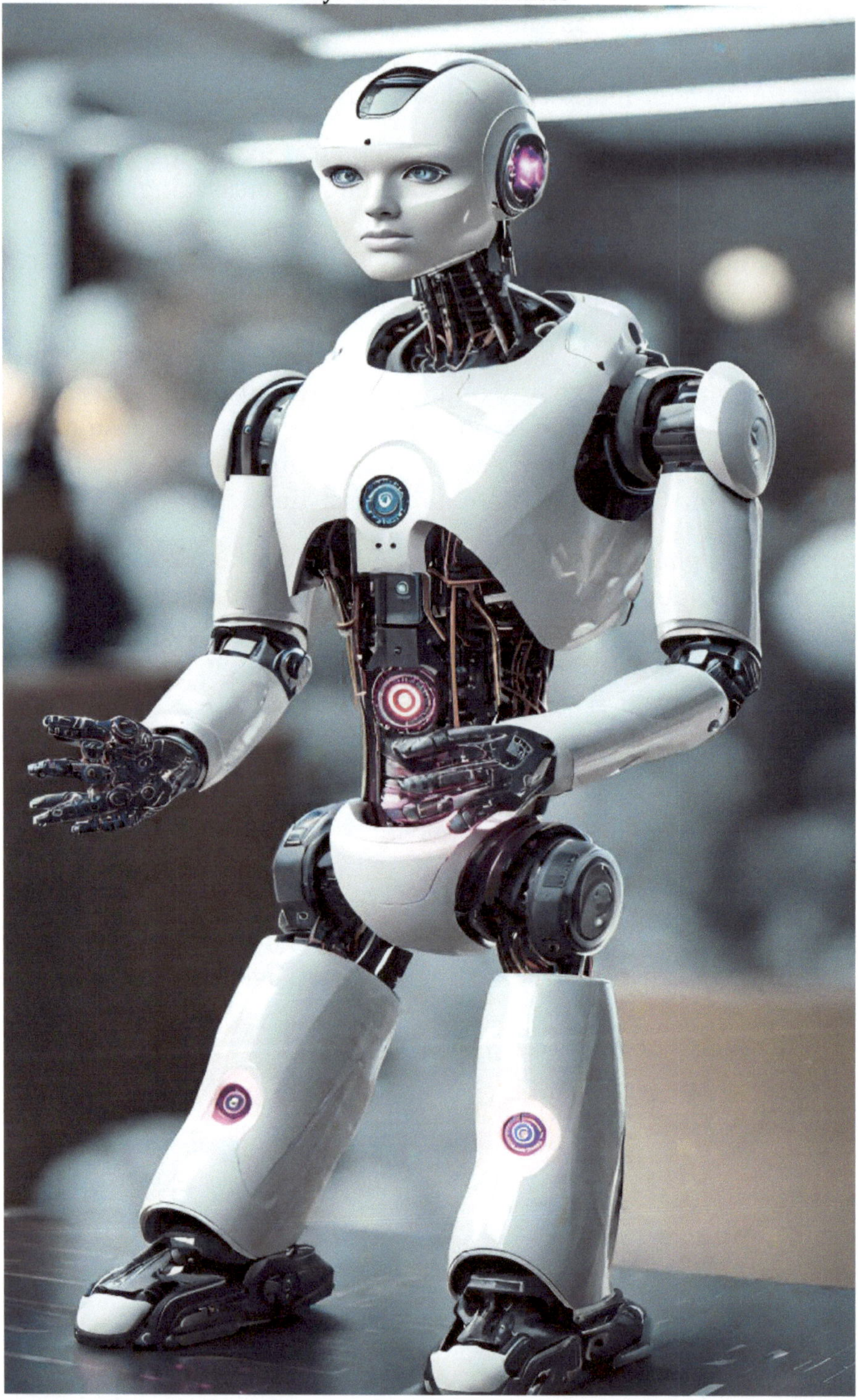

Utilizing AI for Personalized Recommendations and Targeted Advertising

Artificial intelligence (AI) is reshaping the landscape of marketing and customer engagement in ways never before seen. Gone are the days of relying solely on demographic data and broad assumptions about consumer behavior. With the power of AI-driven analytics, businesses can delve deep into the vast amounts of unstructured data available to gain nuanced insights into individual preferences, behaviors, and patterns.

Through advanced machine learning algorithms, AI can process and analyze complex data sets in real-time, providing businesses with a comprehensive understanding of their customers' journey across multiple touchpoints. By identifying key trends, correlations, and anomalies within the data, businesses can uncover hidden opportunities for personalization and targeted marketing strategies that speak directly to each customer's unique needs and desires.

Predictive analytics, another powerful application of AI, enables businesses to forecast future customer behavior with a high degree of accuracy. By leveraging historical data and sophisticated modeling techniques, AI algorithms can anticipate trends, identify potential bottlenecks in the customer journey, and optimize marketing campaigns for maximum impact.

In the realm of customer service, AI-driven chatbots and virtual assistants are revolutionizing the way businesses interact with their customers. These intelligent systems can provide instant, round-the-clock support, answer inquiries, resolve issues, and even initiate sales conversations, all without the need for human intervention. By streamlining customer interactions and improving response times, businesses can enhance customer satisfaction and loyalty while freeing up resources for more strategic initiatives.

Moreover, AI's ability to automate routine marketing tasks, such as campaign management, lead scoring, and content personalization, allows businesses to operate more efficiently and effectively. By reducing manual workload and human error, AI-powered automation systems can increase productivity, scalability, and ROI, ultimately driving business growth and competitive advantage in a rapidly evolving digital landscape.

In conclusion, the transformative power of artificial intelligence in marketing and customer engagement cannot be overstated. By harnessing the full potential of AI-driven analytics, predictive insights, and automation, businesses can unlock new horizons of customer understanding and engagement, paving the way for sustainable growth and success in the dynamic world of modern business.

The Influence of Artificial Intelligence on Business Strategy

Artificial intelligence (AI) has undeniably become a cornerstone of modern business strategies, offering unprecedented opportunities for companies to optimize their operations, drive customer engagement, revolutionize marketing tactics, and fuel innovation across industries. The profound impact of AI on business strategy is reshaping the way organizations operate, adapt, and compete in an increasingly digital and data-driven landscape.

In terms of operational efficiency, AI's ability to analyze vast amounts of data at lightning speed, identify patterns, and make data-driven decisions has empowered businesses to streamline processes, automate workflows, and enhance overall productivity. By leveraging AI-powered predictive analytics, organizations can anticipate market trends, forecast demand, and optimize supply chain operations, ultimately reducing costs, minimizing risks, and maximizing operational efficiency.

Customer engagement stands at the forefront of AI-driven business strategy, as companies strive to deliver personalized and seamless experiences that resonate with their target audiences. AI-enabled chatbots, virtual assistants, and recommendation engines have transformed customer interactions by providing instant support, personalized recommendations, and seamless transactions. This level of real-time engagement not only enhances customer satisfaction but also nurtures brand loyalty and advocacy, driving long-term business success.

The transformative impact of AI is most pronounced in marketing strategies, where businesses are leveraging AI algorithms to analyze consumer behavior, tailor content, and optimize campaigns for maximum impact. By harnessing AI for targeted advertising, dynamic pricing, and personalized communications, organizations can create hyper-targeted campaigns that resonate with individual preferences and drive higher conversion rates. This data-driven approach to marketing allows companies to connect with customers on a personal level, deepening engagement and driving long-term brand loyalty.

In the realm of product development and innovation, AI is driving unprecedented levels of agility, efficiency, and creativity. By harnessing AI-powered tools for market research, trend analysis, and product design, businesses can identify emerging opportunities, innovate rapidly, and bring products to market faster than ever before. The ability to leverage AI for data-driven insights, predictive modeling, and continuous experimentation enables companies to stay ahead of the competition, meet evolving customer needs, and foster a culture of innovation that fuels sustainable growth and success.

In conclusion, the integration of AI into business strategy represents a fundamental shift in how organizations operate, compete, and succeed in today's dynamic business landscape. By embracing AI-driven solutions to optimize operations, enhance customer experiences, drive targeted marketing campaigns, and fuel innovation, businesses can unlock new opportunities, achieve operational excellence, and secure a competitive edge in an era defined by technological disruption and digital transformation. The strategic adoption of AI is not just a strategic advantage but a necessity for businesses looking to thrive, adapt, and lead in a world where data-driven insights and intelligent technologies are reshaping the future of business.

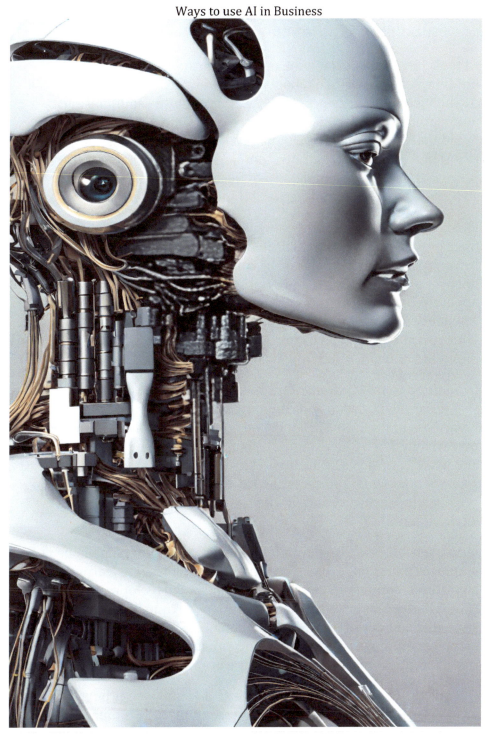

Enhancing Employee Productivity with AI Tools

AI tools have transformed the modern workplace, revolutionizing how employees work, collaborate, and innovate. One of the key ways AI enhances employee productivity is through streamlining and automating repetitive tasks that were once time-consuming and mundane. By leveraging technologies like robotic process automation (RPA) and intelligent chatbots, companies can automate routine processes, freeing up employees to focus on more complex and strategic tasks that require critical thinking and creativity.

Furthermore, AI empowers employees with valuable insights derived from vast amounts of data. Through advanced analytics and machine learning algorithms, AI platforms can analyze complex datasets to uncover patterns, trends, and correlations that may not be readily apparent to human analysis. This data-driven decision-making capability equips employees with the information they need to make informed choices quickly and confidently, ultimately leading to improved outcomes and organizational success.

In addition to task automation and data analysis, AI tools facilitate seamless collaboration and communication among employees, regardless of their physical location. Virtual collaboration platforms powered by AI enable teams to collaborate in real-time, share files, and manage projects efficiently. This virtual workspace fosters a sense of teamwork and camaraderie, crucial for maintaining a strong organizational culture and driving productivity in a digital work environment.

Moreover, AI tools also play a fundamental role in personalizing the employee experience. By leveraging data and machine learning algorithms, companies can tailor learning and development programs, career paths, and performance evaluations to individual employees' strengths and preferences. This personalized approach not only enhances employee engagement and satisfaction but also maximizes their potential and contribution to the organization.

Overall, the transformative impact of AI on employee productivity is vast and multifaceted. By automating tasks, providing data-driven insights, fostering collaboration, and personalizing the employee experience, AI empowers employees to work more efficiently, strategically, and innovatively. As organizations continue to embrace AI technologies, they unlock a wealth of benefits that drive workforce performance and success in an increasingly digital and dynamic business landscape.

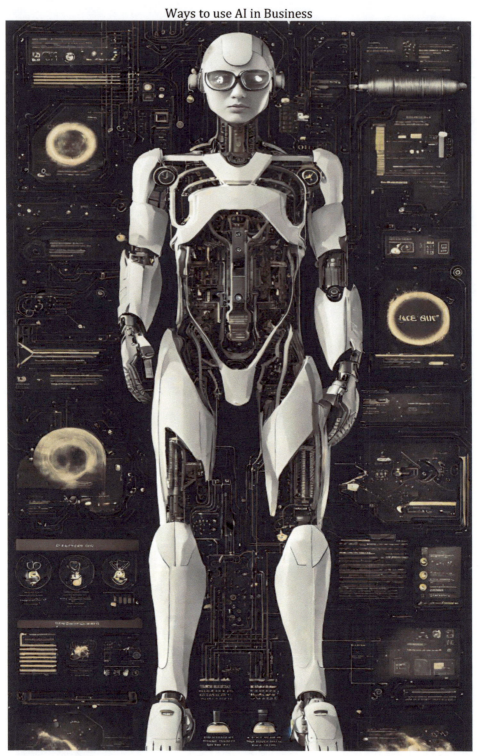

Ensuring Regulatory Compliance in AI Implementation

As we delve deeper into the intricate realm of artificial intelligence (AI) and its intersection with regulatory compliance, the stakes for businesses have never been higher. The rapid advancement of AI technologies brings a myriad of opportunities, but also introduces a host of complex compliance challenges that cannot be ignored.

In an era where data has emerged as the new currency, organizations must navigate a labyrinth of legal frameworks to safeguard individuals' privacy and uphold ethical standards. The onus is on businesses to strike a delicate balance between innovation and compliance, with data protection regulations such as the General Data Protection Regulation (GDPR), California Consumer Privacy Act (CCPA), and sector-specific guidelines like the Health Insurance Portability and Accountability Act (HIPAA) serving as key pillars in this regulatory landscape.

Compliance with these laws is not merely a matter of ticking boxes; it is a strategic imperative that influences consumer trust, operational efficiency, and competitive advantage. Organizations that proactively address compliance requirements position themselves as stewards of data privacy and ethical AI practices, setting a gold standard for industry peers and earning the loyalty of customers who value their privacy rights.

At the heart of compliance in the AI realm lies the need for comprehensive risk assessments. Understanding the data flows, processing activities, and potential vulnerabilities within AI systems is essential to preemptively address compliance gaps and fortify defenses against unforeseen risks. By conducting regular audits and assessments, organizations can identify areas of improvement, implement corrective measures, and demonstrate a robust compliance posture to regulators and stakeholders alike.

Security emerges as a linchpin in the compliance narrative, with data breaches and cyber threats posing significant risks to organizational integrity and regulatory adherence. Leveraging cutting-edge cybersecurity measures, encryption protocols, and access controls is crucial in safeguarding sensitive data and preserving the trust of customers and partners. Organizations must adopt a proactive approach to cybersecurity, implementing threat detection mechanisms, incident response plans, and employee training programs to fortify their defenses against ever-evolving cyber threats.

In the pursuit of compliance excellence, transparency and fairness take center stage. The opacity of AI algorithms and decision-making processes poses ethical dilemmas and regulatory challenges that organizations must address head-on. By embracing algorithmic transparency, conducting impact assessments, and proactively mitigating biases, organizations can uphold fairness and accountability in their AI systems, aligning their practices with regulatory expectations and societal values.

Ethical considerations serve as the moral compass guiding organizations in their AI compliance journey. Recognizing the profound impact of AI on individuals, communities, and societies at large, organizations must embed ethical principles into their AI strategies, from design to deployment. By cultivating a culture of responsible AI innovation, ethical decision-making, and stakeholder engagement, organizations can not only meet compliance mandates but also pave the way for a sustainable, inclusive, and ethically-driven AI ecosystem that benefits all stakeholders, now and in the future.

Addressing Ethical and Privacy Considerations in AI Implementation

In the realm of artificial intelligence (AI) deployment within organizational frameworks, the critical examination of ethical dimensions and the prioritization of privacy considerations are paramount in ensuring the responsible utilization of such advanced technologies. As AI systems continue to advance in sophistication and become integral components of business processes, there is a pressing need for transparency, accountability, and ethical reflection in their deployment.

One of the most prominent ethical dilemmas surrounding the implementation of AI technology pertains to bias. AI algorithms are trained on historical data, which often contains inherent biases and prejudices. If left unchecked, these biases can perpetuate discrimination and inequality, leading to unjust outcomes for certain individuals or groups. Organizations must proactively address bias in AI systems by scrutinizing and diversifying training data sets, employing bias detection tools, and implementing bias mitigation strategies to ensure fair and equitable decision-making processes.

Privacy concerns also loom large in the context of AI integration in business operations. AI systems inherently rely on vast amounts of data to generate insights and predictions, raising significant questions about the protection of individual privacy rights. Organizations must enact robust data protection measures, such as anonymization, encryption, and secure data sharing protocols, to safeguard sensitive information from unauthorized access or misuse. Compliance with regulatory frameworks, such as the General Data Protection Regulation (GDPR) in the European Union, is essential to uphold data privacy standards and foster trust among stakeholders.

Establishing clear governance frameworks and policies governing the ethical use of AI technologies is fundamental in navigating the complex ethical and privacy considerations that accompany AI implementation. Organizations should prioritize transparency by communicating openly with stakeholders about the rationale behind AI deployments, the data sources utilized, and the potential ethical implications of AI-driven decision-making. Regular auditing and monitoring of AI systems to assess their impact on ethical and privacy considerations is crucial for identifying and rectifying potential ethical pitfalls or privacy breaches.

By embracing a proactive approach to ethics and privacy in AI adoption, businesses can not only mitigate risks and potential harm but also cultivate a culture of responsibility, integrity, and trust within their organizations. Prioritizing ethical and privacy considerations in AI deployment is not just a regulatory obligation but a strategic imperative for fostering sustainable relationships with customers, employees, and the broader public in an era defined by technological innovation and ethical scrutiny.

The Future of AI in Business: Trends and Predictions

In the fast-evolving landscape of artificial intelligence (AI) in business, there are several key trends and predictions shaping the future of this technology. One prominent area of focus is the importance of AI ethics and responsible AI practices. As AI capabilities continue to advance, there is a growing awareness of the ethical considerations that come with its use. Issues such as bias in algorithms, data privacy, and the potential societal impact of AI systems are at the forefront of discussions within the business community. To navigate these complexities, businesses must prioritize ethical guidelines and ensure that their AI systems are developed and deployed in a responsible manner.

One crucial aspect of AI ethics is the need for transparency and accountability in AI decision-making processes. As AI systems become increasingly autonomous and make decisions that impact individuals and societies, it is essential for businesses to provide clear explanations of how these decisions are reached. This transparency not only helps build trust with stakeholders but also enables organizations to identify and mitigate potential biases or errors in AI algorithms. By implementing mechanisms for accountability, such as regular audits and oversight committees, businesses can demonstrate their commitment to ethical AI practices and ensure that their systems operate within ethical boundaries.

Another significant trend in the realm of AI in business is the rise of AI-driven automation and augmentation. AI technologies are being leveraged to automate repetitive tasks, streamline workflows, and enhance productivity across various business functions. By deploying AI solutions for automation, organizations can reduce manual workloads, minimize errors, and accelerate decision-making processes. Moreover, AI-driven augmentation tools empower employees with valuable insights and recommendations, enabling them to make more informed decisions and achieve better outcomes. This combination of automation and augmentation not only improves operational efficiency but also enhances the overall performance and agility of businesses in an increasingly competitive market landscape.

Furthermore, the future of AI in business will be characterized by a heightened emphasis on delivering personalized customer experiences and implementing hyper-targeted marketing strategies. AI algorithms have the capacity to analyze vast amounts of customer data to generate tailored recommendations, predict future behavior, and optimize marketing campaigns for specific audience segments. By harnessing the power of AI for personalization, businesses can create more engaging and meaningful interactions with customers, foster brand loyalty, and drive revenue growth. Through the effective use of AI-driven customer insights, organizations can gain a competitive edge in the marketplace by offering unique and customized experiences that resonate with individual preferences and needs.

As AI technologies continue to evolve and expand their applications, businesses must proactively invest in AI capabilities and cultivate a culture of innovation and adaptability. By embracing ethical AI practices, leveraging automation and augmentation tools, and prioritizing personalized customer experiences, organizations can harness the full potential of AI technology to drive sustainable growth and success. In a rapidly changing business environment, businesses that embrace AI as a strategic asset and prioritize ethical considerations will be well-positioned to thrive and lead in the digital era.

www.ingramcontent.com/pod-product-compliance
Lightning Source LLC
La Vergne TN
LVHW072052060326
832903LV00054B/413